INTRODUCING THE STAR OF THIS BOOK

★ ANKYLOSAURUS ★

(an-KY-loh-SAW-russ)

Ankylosaurus means "fused or stiff lizard"

'THE WALKING TANK'

DID YOU KNOW...

that *Ankylosaurus* is famous for being one of the most heavily armoured dinosaurs, built like a tank! It was really well protected, even from the scariest of hungry carnivores (meat eaters), except for one weak spot... more about that later!

SETTING THE SCENE

It all started around 231 million years ago (mya), when the first dinosaurs appeared, part-way through the Triassic Period.

The Age of the Dinosaurs had begun, a time when dinosaurs would rule the world!

Scientists call this time the

MESOZOIC ERA
(mez-oh-zoh-ic)

and this era was so long that they divided it into three periods.

TRIASSIC
lasted 51 million years

JURASSIC
lasted 56 million years

252 million years ago

201 million years ago

Ankylosaurus lived during the Cretaceous Period from 68 – 66 million years ago.

CRETACEOUS
lasted **79** million years

145 million years ago   **66** million years ago

WEATHER REPORT

The world didn't always look like it does today. Before the dinosaurs and during the early part of the Mesozoic Era the land was all stuck together in one supercontinent called Pangaea. Over time, things changed and by the end of the Cretaceous Period the land looked like this.

CRETACEOUS 66 mya
Name comes from the Latin word for 'chalk'

TRIASSIC

Very hot, dry and dusty

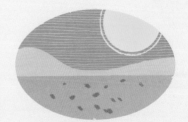

JURASSIC

Hot, humid and tropical

CRETACEOUS

Warm, wet and seasonal

During the Cretaceous Period the continents separated further and the world looked almost like it does today

HOMETOWN

Here's what's been discovered so far and where...

WHAT'S BEEN DISCOVERED:

x5 PARTIAL SKELETONS

PALAEONTOLOGIST
BARNUM BROWN
NAMED ANKYLOSAURUS
IN 1908

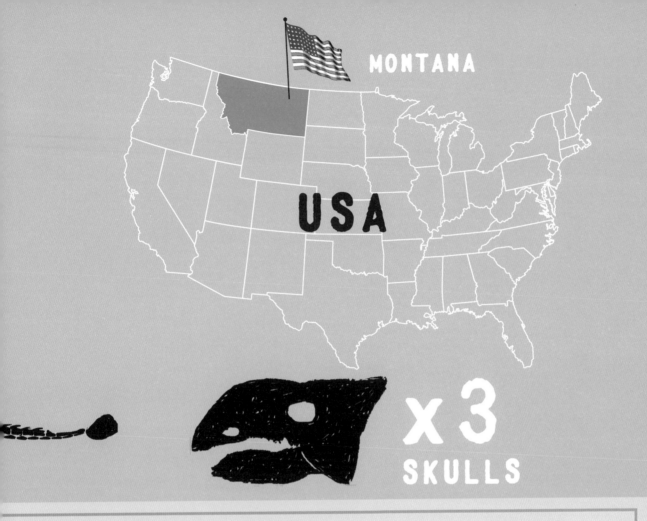

MONTANA

USA

x3
SKULLS

The first fossil was discovered in the Hell Creek Formation in Montana by a team led by a very famous palaeontologist called Barnum Brown, known to his friends as 'Mr Bones'. Other specimens of *Ankylosaurus* have been found in Wyoming, USA and Alberta, Canada.

Although it is the most popular of the armoured dinosaurs, *Ankylosaurus* fossils are quite rare. In fact, many bones, such as the pelvis, tail and feet are yet to be discovered!

VITAL STATISTICS

Some of the earliest dinosaurs that lived on Earth were small and lightly built. Many of the giants came later and *Ankylosaurus* lived alongside them!

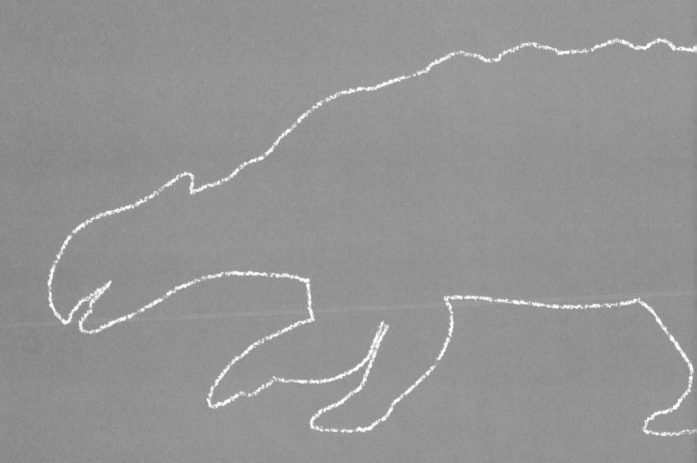

Let's look at *Ankylosaurus* and see what's special, quirky and downright amazing about this dinosaur!

Door
2 m high

Ankylosaurus would have got stuck trying to walk through a single door! It would have needed two doors, side-by-side to walk through as *Ankylosaurus* was a very wide dinosaur.

ANKYLOSAURUS

Length: **6.25 m to 9 m**
Height: **1.7 m – 2 m**
Width: **1.5 m**
Weight: **5 – 6 tonnes**

BUS Traditional double decker

4.5 m high 11 m long 8 tonnes (empty) 2.5 m wide

11

MOUSE   ELEPHANT   Average African elephant

3.5 m high 6 m long 5 tonnes

SCARY
SCALE

How does
Ankylosaurus rate?

NOT SCARY

| 1 | 2 | 3 | 4 | 5 |

On a normal
day when
eating and
chilling

AHHHHHHHH!!!

↑
T. rex is
off the scale!

SCARY

6	7	8	9	10

↑
If attacked no dinosaur
would want to get in the
way of the club on the end
of an *Ankylosaurus* tail!

BRAININESS

When dinosaurs were first discovered
they were thought to be quite stupid!

Then a few scientists thought that some dinosaurs had
a second brain close to their butt! That's now just a myth.

Today scientists know that dinosaurs had one brain and were
intelligent for reptiles. Some were among the most intelligent
creatures alive during the Mesozoic Era, although
still not as smart as most modern mammals.

By looking at the:

Body size

Size
of the
brain

Sense
of
smell

Eyesight

Scientists can tell how they rated against each other...

WHERE DOES ANKYLOSAURUS, A PLANT-EATING DINOSAUR, STAND ON THE 'BRAINY SCALE'?

TROODON
(TRU-oh-don)

10/10
CARNIVORE

ALLOSAURUS
(AL-oh-SAW-russ)

8/10
CARNIVORE

IGUANODON
(ig-WAHN-oh-DON)

6/10
HERBIVORE

STEGOSAURUS
(STEG-oh-SAW-russ)

4/10
HERBIVORE

ANKYLOSAURUS
(an-KIE-loh-SAW-russ)

3/10
HERBIVORE

DIPLODOCUS
(DIP-lod-oh-CUSS)

2/10
HERBIVORE

These dinosaurs are drawn to
scale in relation to each other!

SPEED-O-METER

Ankylosaurus was slow but well protected

S L O W

1 2 3 4 5

6 7 8 9 10

FAST

WEAPONS 9/10

Being slow and heavy meant that some of the dinosaurs needed all the help they could get to survive an attack from some of the scariest creatures ever to walk the Earth!

Ankylosaurus was nicknamed the 'Walking Tank' but its name actually means 'fused or stiff lizard'. This is because of the armour which covered most of its body, making it one of the best protected dinosaurs.

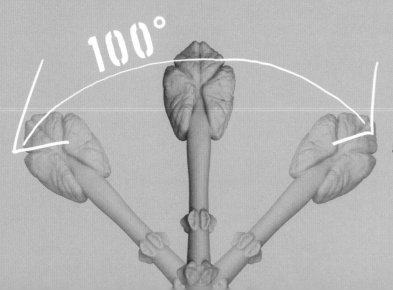
100°

The club was made up of vertebrae fused (stuck) together, which made it a powerful weapon. It was capable of breaking bones and was almost as big as its skull. So far only one tail club has been discovered.

HERE ARE THE SPECIAL BITS THAT ANKYLOSAURUS HAD TO HELP IT STAY ALIVE...

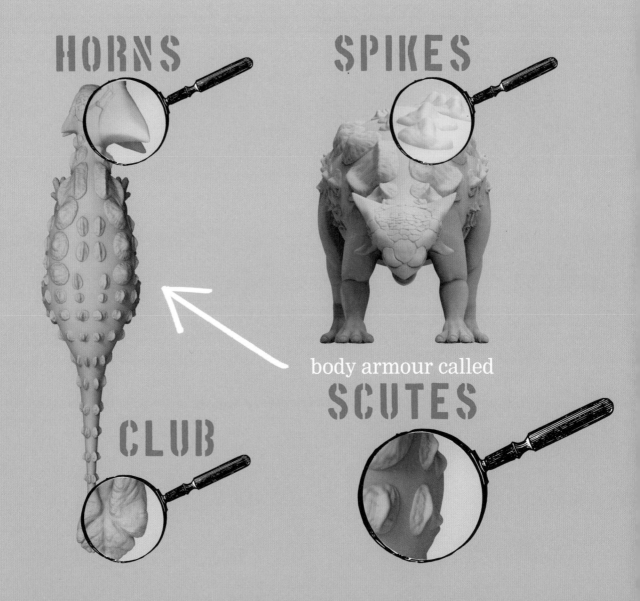

HORNS

SPIKES

CLUB

body armour called

SCUTES

TEETH

You can tell a lot about a dinosaur just by looking at its teeth. Let's look at what kind of teeth *Ankylosaurus* had and what food it ate.

Its small, leaf shaped teeth were great for nipping at leaves, but as *Ankylosaurus* had a limited ability to chew, it probably swallowed much of its food whole.

This tooth is drawn to scale and at just 1 cm high you can see how tiny the teeth of this huge plant-eating dinosaur were compared to the size of its body!

 1 cm Tooth to scale

Over-sized version of the tooth so you can see the detail

DIET

With so much body armour it would not have been able to lift its heavy neck far from the ground, so *Ankylosaurus* would have eaten the low-lying plants and ferns.

As *Ankylosaurus* didn't chew its food properly it probably had a special place in its stomach to help digest the tough plants. This had a side effect, lots and lots of gas... smelly!

Many dinosaurs didn't have any grinding teeth, so like some modern-day birds and reptiles, they would swallow rocks to help digest their food. These rocks are called gastroliths.

WHO LIVED IN THE SAME NEIGHBOURHOOD?

Recently discovered in the Hell Creek Formation, South Dakota, *Dakotaraptor* is one of the largest dromaeosaurs ('raptors') discovered to date.

This claw is life-sized. Scary!

Its large curved foot-claw was a lethal weapon, making this 5 m long dinosaur a perfect killing machine.

DAKOTARAPTOR
(dak-oh-tah-rap-tor)

Living in the same area as *Ankylosaurus*, it was definitely a raptor to avoid!

TYRANNOSAURUS REX

(tie-RAN-oh-SAW-russ rex)

The infamous *T. rex* had a jaw strong enough to crush a car (had cars been invented back then). The ultimate bone cruncher might have tried to flip over an *Ankylosaurus*, not an easy thing to do but *T. rex* was aiming for its one weak spot, its soft underbelly! *Ankylosaurus* would crouch down to try and avoid being flipped!

WHICH ANIMALS ALIVE TODAY ARE MOST LIKE ANKYLOSAURUS?

Ankylosaurus had a hard top and a soft underbelly, just like the giant tortoises that live on the Galapagos Islands today.

- THE LARGEST GIANT TORTOISE WAS 1.5 M LONG

- GIANT ARMADILLOS HAVE REACHED UP TO 1 M

Armadillos live in Central and South America today. They are covered in lots of bony plates which overlap like a roof tile.

This makes the protective layer flexible but very hard to stab or bite through, just like the body armour of an *Ankylosaurus*.

WHAT'S SO SPECIAL ABOUT ANKYLOSAURUS?

WHEN ANKYLOSAURUS LIVED

CRETACEOUS 68 - 66 mya

TOOTH SIZE

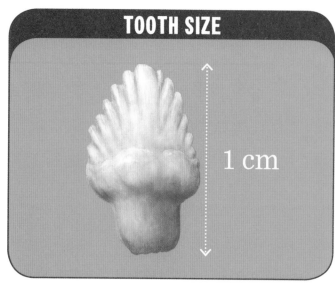

1 cm

WEIGHT

6 TONNES

FAST OR SLOW?

SPEED

2 out of 10

THE BEST BITS!

DISCOVERED, SO FAR

x**5** PARTIAL SKELETONS

x**3** SKULLS

HOW FRIGHTENING?

SCARY

2 if chilling

7 if attacked

MEAT OR PLANTS?

SPECIAL BITS

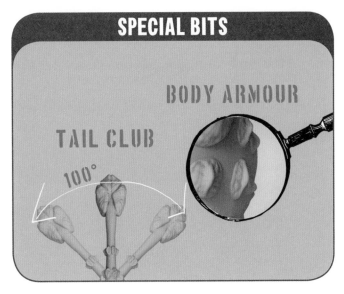

BODY ARMOUR

TAIL CLUB

100°

WHAT'S NEXT ?

OTHER EXCITING TITLES AVAILABLE NOW!

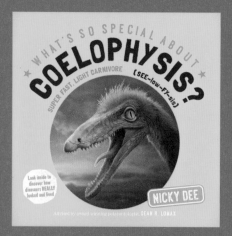

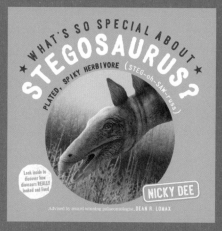

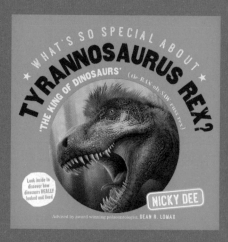

COELOPHYSIS
super-fast, light carnivore;
the first skull to travel
into space!

STEGOSAURUS
plated, spiky
herbivore

T. REX
the 'King of the
Dinosaurs', the ultimate
bone cruncher

COMING SOON

Megalosaurus
the very first dinosaur
to be named

Triceratops
horned and frilled with
a massive skull

Diplodocus
long necked, whip-
tailed giant

Leaellynasaura
tiny, bug-eyed, long
tailed Australian

Join the 'What's So Special Club'

JOIN OUR FREE CLUB

 Download fun dinosaur quizzes and colouring-in sheets
www.specialdinosaurs.com

 Enter the exciting world of a 3D artist and discover how a 3D dinosaur is created and made to look real!

 Find out more about our experts and when they first became fascinated by dinosaurs.

 Who is Nicky Dee? Meet the author online.

 Join the club and be the first to hear about exciting new books, activities and games.

 Club members will be first in line to order new books in the series!

Copyright Published in 2016
by The Dragonfly Group Ltd

email info@specialdinosaurs.com
website www.specialdinosaurs.com

First printed in 2016
Copyright © Nicky Dee 2016
Nicky Dee has asserted her right under the
Copyright, Designs, and Patents Act 1988 to be
identified as the Author of this work.

ISBN: 978-0-9935293-0-6

Printed in China

ACKNOWLEDGEMENTS

Dean R. Lomax
talented, multiple award-winning
palaeontologist, author and science
communicator and the consultant
for the series.
www.deanrlomax.co.uk

David Eldridge
specialist book designer

Gary Hanna
thoroughly talented 3D artist

Scott Hartman
skeletons and silhouettes, professional
palaeoartist and palaeontologist

Ian Durneen
skilled digital sketch artist of the
guest dinosaurs

Ron Blakey
Colorado Plateau Geosystems Inc.
creator of the original
paleogeographic maps

My family
patient, encouraging and wonderfully
supportive. Thank you!

To find out more about our artists, designers
and illustrators please visit the website
www.specialdinosaurs.com